GARLIC

THE GOODNESS OF

GARLIC

40 AMAZING IMMUNE-BOOSTING RECIPES

NATASHA EDWARDS

PHOTOGRAPHY BY PETER CASSIDY

KYLE BOOKS

CONTENTS

GARLIC IS GREAT

How can something so healthy also taste so good? It's a shame we can't say this about all the delicious things in life but happily with garlic, we can as it has both—health benefits and flavor—in abundance. I grew up with garlic—on Mersley Farm, now popularly known as "the garlic farm" on the Isle of Wight—and so inevitably it has played a very big role in my life. And yet, incredibly, years and years of planting, harvesting, cleaning, plaiting, cooking, tasting, and talking about garlic have done nothing to dampen my enthusiasm for the affectionately named "stinking rose". I love garlic and all my family are what you might call devoted "alliophiles". The plant has a natural magnetism: It draws people in, amuses, excites, and inspires and as you are reading this book, it's likely that garlic has already lured you in some way too. Perhaps you already add the odd clove to your cooking or maybe you are intrigued by stories of garlic's therapeutic properties. Whatever your existing relationship with garlic, my mission is to encourage you to use more of it—for its wonderful flavor and its many health benefits too.

PREPARING

The most exciting thing about garlic is how much its flavor varies according to the way it is prepared. Chopping or crushing a raw clove yields that distinctive pungent aroma and tastes strongest.

This is because damaging the clove triggers a powerful chemical reaction that produces allicin, which is largely responsible for garlic's heat and strong smell. For this reason, garlic tastes milder and sweeter when cooked whole.

garlic press will leave less waste and be easier to clean.

Crushing the garlic in a pestle and mortar will achieve a similar flavor but a different consistency. If you cook minced garlic, the flavor becomes milder. The chemical reactions in the clove take up to a minute to occur, so wait before adding minced garlic to the pan or a dressing to get the strongest flavor.

Peeling

Peeling garlic can be fiddly, but the larger and drier the cloves, the easier the job becomes. If you intend to crush the clove for cooking, the easiest way is to lay the blade of a large knife on top of the clove then press down on it with the heel of your hand. This breaks the skin away from the flesh quite easily.

Alternatively, you can buy a small rubber tube that peels the garlic cloves in seconds. Simply put the clove inside the tube, roll on a counter, and apply pressure to release the skin.

Crushing

Crushing garlic releases the maximum allicin and other sulfur-containing compounds from the clove, so it will result in the strongest flavors. There's a huge variety of garlic presses available and most will do an adequate job, but a better-quality

Slicing

Peeled garlic can be easily sliced with a sharp knife. But if you are preparing a large quantity you may want to use a garlic slicer, which is like a mini mandolin. Sliced garlic has a slightly milder flavor than minced garlic. It's great in stirfries and curries and can be lightly fried to create a sweeter, nutty flavor. Take care not to burn the garlic when you fry it though, as the flavor then becomes very bitter.

GARLIC FINGERS

When you're peeling, chopping and slicing cloves, garlic fingers become slightly unavoidable! However, there are a few antidotes you can try.

Some people soak their hands in lemon juice or vinegar, and then wash with warm water and soap, or you can try rubbing your hands against stainless steel, which is often conveniently close at hand in a kitchen. Apparently the molecules from the steel and the garlic bond and remove the smell from your fingers. (This also works for onions.) When you're peeling garlic, you often find some sneaks under your fingernails so I'd definitely recommend a nailbrush.

Green sprout

If your garlic is quite old and has already started to sprout, you may find a small green shoot on the inside of the clove when you cut it open. Although this is completely harmless and will not impair the flavor of the garlic, some people prefer to remove the shoot as it can be difficult to digest.

MEDICINAL MARVEL

Our ancestors intuited that garlic had enormous potential as a natural healer and these days scientific research is proving it all to be true. As well as vitamins and minerals, the cloves contain numerous health-giving sulphur compounds, of which allicin is the most potent. These are triggered into action when a garlic clove is chewed, minced, or cut, releasing its signature pungent aroma. They then set to work in harmony with the body to protect it against a variety of common ailments and more serious diseases. Millions of years of evolution have allowed the garlic bulb to perfect this self-protecting mechanism—all we have to do is consume it!

BUYING THE BEST

In order to enjoy the best flavor in your cooking, it's vital to use good-quality produce. It's great that garlic is so easy to come by these days and the local supermarket almost always has a good supply, though it's worth being aware that the kind of garlic on offer in supermarkets is generally not of the best quality.

Therefore, if you are looking for good-quality, long-lasting, flavorful garlic, it is best to look a little further afield. Growing your own garlic from sound stock is a very good way to ensure an ample supply of fresh bulbs, but farmers' markets, farm shops and online are also good sources, and often offer a wide range of varieties.

Top tips for buying good garlic

◆ Always buy the bulbs intact and without cloves missing. Once the bulb is broken up, its life is shortened.

◆ Test the bulb for firmness—the firmer the cloves, the better. Any softness suggests the bulb is old and either won't last much longer or may already have started to go powdery on the inside.

◆ Avoid any garlic with green shoots. If small green shoots have started to appear at the tip of the cloves, the garlic has already started to sprout. You can still use the garlic, but it won't last as long as a fresher bulb.

HEALTH BURST

Allicin is the source of garlic's goodness and because it is partially destroyed by cooking, you'll get the greatest health boost if you use it raw or slightly cooked. Quite a few of the recipes that follow use garlic in this state and so preserve its optimum health-giving properties. However, don't be afraid that cooking garlic removes all the benefits as in fact it leads to other sulfur compounds being created which are also extremely beneficial to your health.

Storing

The best place to keep garlic is somewhere dry, at room temperature, and somewhere with good air circulation. Alternatively, store bulbs in a pot with ventilation holes. Avoid plastic to prevent mold. Only store green garlic in the refrigerator and do not freeze green or dry garlic as the texture will change. Properly stored garlic can last for months.

STARTERS & SOUPS

GARLIC & TOMATO TARTE TATIN *VEGETARIAN

This variation on the traditional tarte tatin melts in the mouth and makes an impressive dinner-party starter or summer lunch dish.

Serves 6

For the caramelized garlic
3 to 4 garlic bulbs, cloves peeled
Olive oil
1 tablespoon balsamic vinegar
2 teaspoons light brown sugar
Sprig each of rosemary and thyme, finely chopped
1 teaspoon salt

For the tomatoes
Olive oil
4 ripe plum tomatoes, cut lengthwise (or a basket of ripe cherry tomatoes, halved)
3 teaspoons light brown sugar
Salt and freshly ground black pepper

For the pastry
Ready-rolled puff pastry sheet, cut to fit over an 8-inch ovenproof frying pan
1 egg, beaten

To garnish
½ pound feta cheese, crumbled
Sprigs of thyme

1. Preheat the oven to 375°F.

2. Put the garlic cloves in a small pan with water to cover and bring to a boil. Boil for 3 minutes then drain and dry the cloves and the pan. Return the garlic to the pan along with a glug of olive oil and fry for another 3 minutes. Add 1 cup of water and the balsamic vinegar and boil for 10 minutes, or until most of the liquid has evaporated.

4. In the meantime, for the tomatoes pour a glug of olive oil onto a large plate and mix in the brown sugar and plenty of salt and pepper. Place the tomatoes, cut side down, into the oil ensuring each face is covered.

5. Heat a small glug of olive oil in the ovenproof frying pan and transfer the tomatoes, cut side down, into the pan. Fry for about 5 minutes, or until they start to go sticky, then remove from the heat.

6. By now most of the liquid should have evaporated from the garlic. Add the sugar, herbs, and salt, and continue to fry until the cloves begin to brown. Remove from the heat then transfer the cloves to the frying pan and arrange around the tomatoes.

7. Place the pastry sheet over the tomatoes and garlic, tucking the edges of the pastry neatly into the pan. Brush with the beaten egg then place in the oven for 25 minutes, or until golden brown. Remove and cool slightly.

8. Take a large heatproof serving plate and place over the pan. Protecting your hands with oven mitts and holding the plate and pan firmly together, carefully flip the pan and the plate, then lift off the pan.

9. Sprinkle with the feta cheese and garnish with a thyme sprig or two. Serve with arugula or watercress.

CEVICHE *DAIRY-FREE

A Latin American classic, ceviche is traditionally made with raw fish marinated in citrus juices and other flavorings, which depend on the regional variation. The acidity of the juice changes the chemical structure of the fish in a similar way to cooking, but leaves it with a wonderfully fresh texture and taste. For me, this dish is all about the incredible "zing" on the palate and so I like to add plenty of chili, garlic and cayenne.

Serves 4 as an appetizer

1 pound sea bass, sole fillets
   or other very fresh
   white fish, skinned
   and deboned
1 small red onion, very
   finely sliced
1 celery stick, very finely
   sliced
1 to 2 red chiles, deseeded
   and finely sliced
1 teaspoon cayenne pepper
2 garlic cloves
Juice of 3 limes
Juice of 1 lemon
A handful of cilantro, coarsely
   chopped
A handful of mint, coarsely
   chopped
Sea salt

1. Make sure the fish fillets are completely bone- and skin-free, then slice them across the grain into ½-inch-thick pieces

2. Place the fish in a large bowl and add the onion, celery, chiles, and cayenne. Crush in the garlic and pour over the citrus juices, carefully turning the ingredients with a wooden spoon to mix them thoroughly. Make sure the fish is completely covered in citrus juice.

3. Place the bowl in the refrigerator for at least 2 hours to allow the fish to "cook" in the marinade. You will be able to tell when it's ready as the fish flesh will have become opaque.

4. Stir through the cilantro and mint, sprinkle with salt and serve immediately on one large sharing plate or in small dishes with the juices from the bottom of the bowl poured over.

GARLIC BLOODY MARY
*VEGETARIAN *DAIRY-FREE

The wicked combination of garlic, tomatoes and vodka makes for a punchy cocktail or "hair-of-the-dog" concoction. Perhaps not the healthiest way to consume your daily dose of garlic, but definitely a fun means of testing the wonder herb's reputation as a hangover cure. Alternatively, omit the vodka and drink your Garlic Virgin Mary guilt-free. Without vodka it's still a great way to increase your raw garlic intake. Prepare ahead and refrigerate overnight to get the best flavors.

Makes 4 tall glasses

3 cups tomato juice
Juice of 1 lemon
Juice of 1 lime
1 tablespoon freshly grated
   horseradish
1 tablespoon Worcestershire
   sauce
2 garlic cloves, minced
1 teaspoon Tabasco
Salt and freshly ground
   black pepper
Premium vodka
Celery sticks and ice cubes,
   to serve

1. Place all the ingredients, apart from the seasoning and vodka, in a blender and combine well. Season to taste then refrigerate until thoroughly chilled. The flavor improves the longer you leave it, so try to leave for at least 1 hour and overnight if possible. This virgin mixture will keep in the refrigerator for a week so.

2. Put a few ice cubes in each glass, pour in an ounce (or two) of vodka, then top with the Garlic Bloody Mary mixture. Alternatively, pour the virgin mixture without the alcohol, either straight or on the rocks. Serve with a stick of celery in each glass.

VIETNAMESE CHICKEN BROTH *DAIRY-FREE

Warming, invigorating, low-fat and incredibly tasty, I love to eat this soup any day; although it's particularly good for anyone with a cold. You can adjust the chile to taste.

Serves 4

3 cups chicken stock
1 sachet instant miso soup
4 garlic cloves
A thumb-sized piece of
    ginger, cut into matchsticks
1 to 2 red chiles, deseeded and
    finely sliced
2 skinless chicken breasts
½ tablespoon sunflower oil
Sea salt and freshly ground
    black pepper
¼ pound egg noodles
2 bok choy, chopped
1 tablespoon soy sauce
Juice of ½ lime
2 scallions, sliced
A large handful of cilantro

1. In a saucepan, heat the stock until simmering then remove from the heat and add the miso, stirring until dissolved. While the stock is still hot, finely chop 2 garlic cloves and add to the stock with all the ginger and chiles. Cover with a lid and leave to infuse.

2. Using a sharp knife, score the chicken breasts deeply three to four times across the top, then brush with sunflower oil and crush a garlic clove over each one, rubbing it into the meat. Fry for a few minutes on each side until browned but not completely cooked through.

3. Place the chicken on a chopping board and slice into strips. Add the chicken, noodles, and chopped bok choy to the infused stock, return to the heat and simmer for a few minutes, until the noodles and chicken are cooked.

4. Add the soy sauce and lime juice and serve immediately in large bowls with some sliced scallion and cilantro on top. Eat with chopsticks for the noodles and a spoon to scoop up the tasty broth.

IMMUNITY-BOOSTING
SOUP *VEGETARIAN *DAIRY-FREE

This clear broth does wonders if you're feeling congested and makes a very effective immune booster too. The large amount of garlic may surprise you, but trust me, the flavor is fantastic. Shiitake mushrooms are a symbol of longevity in Asia and an excellent source of selenium, a known antioxidant that plays a vital role in boosting the immune system.

Serves 4

1 ounce dried shiitake, porcini, and oyster mushrooms (add extra fresh shiitake mushrooms, if available)
1 tablespoon olive oil
1 medium white onion, finely chopped
A thumb-sized piece of ginger, peeled and grated
1 whole garlic bulb, peeled
1 tablespoon vegetable bouillon powder or 1 vegetable stock cube
Juice of 1 lemon
Sea salt and freshly ground black pepper

1. Pour 1 cup of boiling water over the dried mushrooms in a bowl and leave them to soak for 10 minutes.

2. In the meantime, heat the oil in a heavy-based ovenproof pan. Add the onion and ginger then crush in all the garlic cloves. Fry gently until softened and aromatic.

3. Add the mushrooms and their water to the pan, plus any fresh mushrooms, then stir in the stock and the lemon juice.

4. Season then gently simmer with the lid on for at least 2 hours. Alternatively, transfer the pan to a low oven (about 250°F). Season to taste before serving with crusty bread.

GAZPACHO *VEGETARIAN *DAIRY-FREE

Hot summer lunches are an ideal time to serve this very flavorful and refreshing, cold soup. It can be difficult to get raw garlic into your diet and this is an excellent option. If the weather is very hot, or if you haven't had time to chill the soup well, you can just add a few ice cubes before serving, as the Spaniards do.

Serves 6

2 pounds very ripe, good-quality tomatoes, coarsely chopped
2 scallions, chopped
3 garlic cloves
1 large cucumber, chopped
3 tablespoons olive oil
Juice of 1 lemon
2 tablespoons sherry vinegar
A handful of fresh basil leaves, finely chopped
A few stems of fresh flat-leaf parsley, finely chopped

For the garnish
2 slices of white bread, cubed
Olive oil, for frying
½ red pepper, finely diced
Cucumber, finely diced
Salt and freshly ground black pepper

1. Put the tomatoes, scallions, garlic, and most of the cucumber (retain a small amount for the garnish) into a blender and blend until smooth. Pass through a fine sieve to remove most of the pulp.

2. Put the mixture back in the blender and slowly add the olive oil, lemon juice, and sherry vinegar until combined before adding the basil and parsley. Be careful not to blend the herbs for too long as you want them to remain finely chopped, not puréed. Chill in the refrigerator.

3. To make the garnish, gently fry the bread in a little olive oil to make croûtons. To serve, season the gazpacho well before transferring to bowls and topping with the chopped vegetables and croûtons.

The secret to a great gazpacho is to use really ripe, premium tomatoes. Big, plump, fleshy ones are the best as they have fewer seeds, but anything sweet and delicious will help to produce a tasty soup.

BRUSCHETTA

This classic Italian antipasto is a delicious and simple way to include raw garlic in your diet. Any good-quality, fresh bread can be used, though I prefer ciabatta, and you can try adding different toppings, such as pesto, cheese, anchovies, cured meats or grilled vegetables.

Serves 4

1 small ciabatta loaf, cut diagonally into 1-inch slices
Extra virgin olive oil
4 garlic cloves, peeled
6 very ripe vine tomatoes, diced
A small handful of fresh basil leaves, torn
Sea salt and freshly ground black pepper

1. Brush each side of the ciabatta slices with olive oil then toast under the grill on both sides.

2. While the bread is still hot, rub with the raw garlic cloves, top with the chopped tomatoes and basil leaves then drizzle with olive oil and season well.

GARLIC, ONION, & THYME FRITTATA

*VEGETARIAN *GLUTEN-FREE

This flavorful Italian omelet borrows potatoes from the Spanish tortilla, and is delicious as an antipasto or a simple Sunday-night dinner. Serve with a fresh, crunchy salad, drizzled with classic vinaigrette (see page 78).

*Serves 4 as a main
or 6 as an antipasto*

2 large potatoes, peeled and sliced to ½ inch thick
2 tablespoons olive oil
2 tablespoons butter
4 small onions, or 2 large, thinly sliced
A large handful of fresh thyme sprigs, leaves only, plus extra sprigs to garnish
3 garlic cloves
6 eggs
Salt and freshly ground black pepper

1. Bring a pan of salted water to a boil and blanch the sliced potatoes for 3 minutes. Take care not to overcook them or they will fall apart in the frying pan. Drain in a colander to allow the steam to escape and set aside.

2. Heat the oil and butter in a non-stick frying pan then add the onions and fry over low heat for 5 minutes, stirring occasionally. Add the thyme leaves, crush in the garlic with a pinch of salt and cook for another 2 minutes.

3. Add the potatoes to the pan, carefully turning them to coat in the oil and butter. Add more oil if necessary. Cook for another 5 minutes on medium heat.

4. Meanwhile, beat the eggs with a good pinch of salt and some freshly ground black pepper then pour the egg mixture into the pan.

5. Cook on low heat until the frittata starts to come away from the sides of the pan, then place the pan under the grill until the top of the frittata has browned slightly. The perfect frittata should be golden brown on the outside and slightly soft inside.

6. Serve the frittata directly from the pan or, if you're feeling confident, slide it out of the pan onto a plate and garnish with a couple of thyme sprigs.

AVOCADO GARLIC
SHRIMP *GLUTEN-FREE

This combination is packed full of goodness and makes a very easy starter or lunch dish.

Serves 4

2 tablespoons butter
1 pound raw fresh shrimp,
    peeled, deveined
3 garlic cloves
1 tablespoon sweet chile sauce
2 ripe avocados, peeled,
    halved, stones removed
Juice of 1 lemon
Salt and freshly ground black
    pepper
A bunch of fresh chives,
    finely chopped, to garnish

1. Heat the butter in a heavy-based frying pan or wok on high heat. Throw in the shrimp, quickly crush in the garlic, then stir until the shrimp are cooked through. Once cooked, stir through the sweet chile sauce.

2. Place half an avocado on each plate and top with the cooked shrimp. Squeeze plenty of lemon juice over the shrimp, season with salt and freshly ground pepper then sprinkle with chopped chives.

ZUCCHINI FRITTERS

*DAIRY-FREE

These are best made with fresh zucchini as they give off less water. If your grated zucchini seem watery, sprinkle them with salt and leave for 15 minutes. Then place them in a clean tea towel and wring out some of the liquid into the sink.

Serves 4 as a starter

2 medium zucchini, grated
1 cup grated mozzarella
A handful of fresh mint
  leaves, finely chopped
2 garlic cloves
Salt and freshly ground
  black pepper
¼ cup flour
2 tablespoons olive oil
Sweet chile dipping sauce,
  to serve

1. Place the grated zucchini, mozzarella, and chopped mint into a large bowl. Crush in the garlic cloves, season with salt and freshly ground black pepper, then mix everything together.

2. Add in the flour and 1 tablespoon of olive oil and stir well until the ingredients start to bind. If the mixture seems too wet, add more flour. Shape the mixture into golf-ball-sized pieces, then flatten.

3. Heat the remaining olive oil in a non-stick frying pan over medium heat. Fry the fritters for 2 to 3 minutes on each side until golden brown.

4. Serve immediately with sweet chile dipping sauce.

To maximize garlic's health-promoting potential, leave it for around 10 minutes after you have prepared it, to allow time for the alliin to be converted into allicin while the enzyme is still active.

GARLIC, CUMIN, &
BEET FRITTERS
*VEGETARIAN *DAIRY-FREE *GLUTEN-FREE

The brilliant color of these sweet and delicious mouthfuls make a wonderful starter to serve alongside freshly made tzatziki dip (see page 80) for dunking. Increase the quantities and pile them high for impressive party nibbles.

Makes 12 small fritters

2 teaspoons cumin seeds
4 large raw beets,
    peeled and grated
¼ cup flour, plus extra for
    shaping fritters
2 garlic cloves
Salt and freshly ground
    black pepper
3 tablespoons olive oil
Tzatziki (page 80), to serve

1. Heat a frying pan, add the cumin seeds, and toast over high heat for 2 minutes to release their flavor.

2. In a bowl, combine the grated beets, flour, and cumin seeds then crush in the garlic cloves and sprinkle with salt and pepper.

3. Use your hands to bring all the ingredients together, squeezing the mixture to absorb all the flour.

4. With wet hands, shape the mixture into small balls. (This can be a little awkward, but don't worry; the beets will hold their shape once in the oil.) Sprinkle some flour onto a plate and coat the balls in the flour.

5. Heat the olive oil in a non-stick frying pan over medium heat. Carefully place the beet balls into the pan, fry on each side until crispy then place on paper towels to absorb excess oil.

6. Serve immediately with tzatziki dip.

For a more formal dish, try serving these fritters on individual plates with tzatziki drizzled over the top. Accompany with a small watercress salad on the side. The flavors work perfectly and, it looks beautiful too.

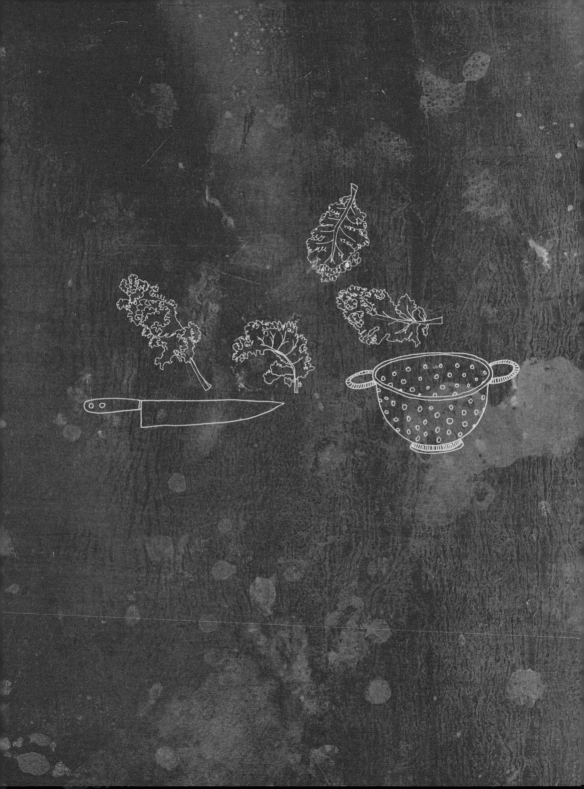

SIDES
& SALADS

OAK-SMOKED GARLIC DAUPHINOISE

*VEGETARIAN *GLUTEN-FREE

I lived in Paris for a few years, sharing an apartment with a Canadian girl who was writing a French cookbook. I gave her smoked garlic from the farm and she loved it, adding a recipe for smoked garlic dauphinoise in her book. Since it's hard to say whether or not smoked garlic has any health benefits, you can substitute it with ordinary garlic if you wish—it adds a great flavor too.

Serves 4 to 6

2 pounds potatoes, thinly sliced

Sea salt and freshly ground black pepper

1 teaspoon freshly grated nutmeg

1 bulb oak-smoked garlic, cloves (or 3 to 4 ordinary garlic cloves), peeled

2 cups homogenized milk or milk mixed with cream

3 tablespoons butter, cut into slivers

1. Preheat the oven to 375°F.

2. Place half the sliced potatoes in a large ovenproof gratin dish. Cover with a layer of seasoning then grate the garlic cloves over the top.

3. Tip the remainder of the potato slices into the dish, spreading them out evenly. Season again then pour in the milk and lay the butter slivers on top.

4. Bake in the oven until all the liquid has been absorbed and the top has browned, about 1 to 1½ hours.

5. Serve with roasted meat and green vegetables.

This dish represents the ultimate comfort food. It's all about the long, slow cooking process so don't rush it. Check the dish halfway through and, if necessary, push the potatoes down so the cream is able to swim over and bubble on top. When it's ready it should be really brown and crispy so make sure it's finished to perfection.

ROASTED GARLIC POTATOES *DAIRY-FREE

Good roasted potatoes are to die for, and once you taste this simple variation, well, you might have to die twice!

Serves 4 to 6

2 pounds new potatoes
¼ cup olive oil
Salt and freshly ground
  black pepper
1 large garlic bulb, separated
  into unpeeled cloves
1 lemon, halved and squeezed
A few sprigs of rosemary,
  leaves only

1. Preheat the oven to 400°F.

2. Bring a large pan of salted water to a boil. Carefully add the potatoes and boil for around 7 minutes, or until they offer no resistance to a knife.

3. Drain the potatoes then cut them in half and return to the pan. Holding a lid on the pan, shake the potatoes around to fluff up the edges. Now toss with the olive oil, salt and freshly ground black pepper, juice of the lemon, and rosemary leaves.

4. Spread the potatoes in a roasting pan and distribute the garlic cloves among them. Add the lemon halves to the pan, then roast for 40 minutes, or until golden brown and crunchy. Discard the lemon halves before serving.

SPICY SPROUTING BROCCOLI
*DAIRY-FREE *GLUTEN-FREE

You can use this as a sauce served with noodles or as an accompaniment to grilled chicken.

Serves 4

1½ pounds sprouting
broccoli or kale
1 heaping teaspoon sesame
seeds
½ tablespoon olive oil
½ tablespoon sesame oil
5 garlic cloves, finely sliced
A thumb-sized piece of
ginger, finely sliced
1 red chile, deseeded and
finely diced
1 tablespoon white wine
vinegar
1 tablespoon light soy sauce

1. Bring a large pan of salted water to a boil. Add the broccoli and blanch for 3 to 4 minutes, then drain and set aside.

2. Meanwhile, heat a small frying pan, add the sesame seeds, and toast over medium heat for 2 minutes until they start to pop. Set aside.

3. In another frying pan, heat the oils over medium heat, then add the garlic, ginger, and chile, and fry gently for 2 minutes.

4. Add the broccoli and coat with the oil mixture. Add the vinegar and soy sauce and cook for another 2 minutes.

5. Serve with the sesame seeds sprinkled over.

For those wishing to reduce their salt intake, garlic makes a great alternative. It adds substantial flavor to your cooking and means you'll need to use far less salt.

SOM TAM *DAIRY-FREE

Any visitor to Thailand will have come across this fantastic, fresh, hot and spicy dish made from green (unripe) papayas. It was my daily lunch when. It's hard to replicate the exact flavors here but this combination comes quite close. Always use unripe papaya, never the ripe (orange) kind.

Serves 4

1 large green papaya, peeled and deseeded (or 1 unripe mango, pitted, or 1 cucumber, deseeded)
5 garlic cloves
3 red chiles, finely chopped (or to taste)
Large pinch of salt
1 teaspoon dried shrimp or shrimp paste
1 tablespoon fish sauce
Juice of 2 limes
1 tablespoon sugar
4 cherry tomatoes, cut into small slices
¼ cup beansprouts
¼ cup crushed peanuts

1. Shred the papaya (or mango or cucumber) into long, thin matchsticks.

2. Using a pestle and mortar, crush the garlic, chiles, and salt. Add a small handful of the papaya and the dried shrimp or shrimp paste and gently pound until some of the juices are released.

3. Transfer to a bowl and stir in the rest of the ingredients, reserving some of the peanuts to sprinkle on top before serving.

The raw freshness of this dish not only gives a beautiful crunchy texture and delicious flavors but also makes it very nutritious. Surprisingly filling and very easy to prepare, it makes a great light lunch alternative to your average sandwich.

WARM LENTIL
& HALLOUMI SALAD
*VEGETARIAN

My idea of heaven. Halloumi never fails to please in this quick and easy way to a delicious, healthy, and filling lunch.

Serves 4

1 cup puy lentils
1 teaspoon vegetable bouillon
  powder
½ red onion, finely sliced
1 green chile, deseeded and
  finely sliced
2 tablespoons olive oil
2 garlic cloves
1 tablespoon olive oil
½ pound halloumi, sliced
2 small zucchini, cut into
  ribbons with a peeler
¼ cup pomegranate seeds
A handful of chopped fresh
  cilantro, including stalks
Sea salt and freshly ground
  black pepper

1. Cover the lentils with cold water and bring to a boil. Add the vegetable bouillon and cook for 15 to 20 minutes, or until the lentils are tender. Drain well.

2. While the lentils are still warm, place them in a large bowl. Add the onion, chile, and olive oil then crush in the garlic cloves and stir well.

3. For the halloumi, heat the oil in a frying pan on medium heat. Add the halloumi and fry on each side until golden. Stir the zucchini, pomegranate seeds, and cilantro into the bowl with the lentils. Season to taste.

4. Top the lentil mixture with the halloumi slices and serve.

You can add garlic to almost any salad, either in a salad dressing or as very thin, lightly fried garlic slices, scattered over as a topping. Take great care not to burn the garlic though as this will make it taste very bitter.

GARLIC & ROSEMARY FOCACCIA *VEGETARIAN *DAIRY-FREE

Focaccia is very easy to make and is always popular with the whole family. My children devour it.

*Makes 1 large
or 2 medium-sized loaves*

3 cups flour, plus extra
  for dusting
¼ ounce (7g) packet fast
  action yeast
1 teaspoon salt
1¾ cup warm water
1 to 2 teaspoons honey
  or sugar
¼ cup olive oil, plus extra
  for oiling
4 garlic cloves
3 sprigs of fresh rosemary,
  leaves only, finely chopped
Sea salt

1. Place the flour, yeast and 1 teaspoon of salt in a large bowl and make a well in the middle.

2. Fill a measuring jug with just over 1¼ cup of warm water and stir in the honey or sugar and olive oil. Pour most of this mixture into the bowl of flour, stirring with a wooden spoon or your fingers to bring the dough together. Add a little more water if necessary until the dough has a soft, slightly wet consistency that is easily workable.

3. Place the dough on a lightly floured counter and knead for at least 10 minutes, until it becomes elastic and smooth.

4. Clean, dry, and oil the bowl before placing the dough back in, then cover with oiled plastic wrap. Let rise in a warm place until it has doubled in size.

5. Preheat the oven to 375°F.

6. Once the dough has risen, knock it back on a clean floured counter. Shape the dough into one or two oval-shaped flat loaves, transfer onto baking pans then let rise again for about 20 minutes.

7. In the meantime, pour 2 tablespoons of olive oil into a small bowl, crush in the garlic cloves, stir in the chopped rosemary and mix well.

8. When the dough has risen, make holes in it with your fingertips then pour over the garlic and rosemary mixture, making sure it gets into the holes.

9. Sprinkle with plenty of sea salt and place in the oven to bake for 30 minutes, or until golden and hollow-sounding when tapped on the bottom. Turn out onto a wire rack to cool.

Including garlic in bread dough itself, I found out the hard way, can impair the dough's ability to rise. This recipe avoids this pitfall by adding the garlic as a topping.

THE BEST CHEESY GARLIC BREAD *VEGETARIAN

Garlic and bread can be combined in a huge variety of ways. We've tried many at the farm and can guarantee this one will be polished off quickly.

Makes 1 baguette

½ cup butter
3 to 4 large garlic cloves
1 cup mozzarella
1 cup Cheddar
A handful of fresh herbs—
parsley, basil, and oregano
all work well
1 fresh baguette, sliced
diagonally at 1- to 2-inch
intervals
Paprika, for sprinkling

1. Preheat the oven to 375°F.

2. Put all the filling ingredients in a blender or food processor and blend.

3. Generously spread the filling between the baguette slices. Wrap the baguette loosely in aluminum foil, then place in the oven for 20 to 25 minutes, until the filling has melted.

4. Remove from the oven, open the foil and sprinkle with paprika. Leaving the foil open, return the baguette to the oven for a few minutes, until the crust is golden brown.

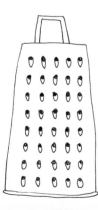

TOASTED CIABATTA

*DAIRY-FREE

At our café, the brilliant chef likes to use the different varieties of garlic we grow to suit different dishes. He recommends strong-flavored Chesnok Wight for this garlic bread.

Makes 2 loaves

½ cup salted butter, softened
3 fat Chesnok Wight cloves, or other strong-flavored garlic variety, finely chopped
1 sprig of fresh rosemary, leaves only, finely chopped
2 ciabatta loaves, cut lengthwise
Chile flakes (optional)

1. Mix the butter with the garlic and rosemary.

2. Spread the ciabatta with a thick layer of garlic butter. Place on a grill tray and grill until golden brown.

3. Cut the toasted ciabatta diagonally and serve. Add a light sprinkling of chile flakes to spice it up if you wish.

MAINS

CHICKEN WITH 40 GARLIC CLOVES

*DAIRY-FREE *GLUTEN-FREE

Happily, some 1970s dinner-party classics are making a comeback, including this traditional French dish, which makes the most of garlic's sweet, rich flavor by cooking the cloves encased in their skins. Once cooked, the cloves can be served as they are, so that guests can squeeze garlic onto their plates. Alternatively, use the extracted flesh to create a deliciously creamy sauce.

Serves 4 to 6

2 celery stalks, chopped
1 large organic chicken
   (about 3½ pounds)
2 large sprigs of rosemary
2 large sprigs of thyme
3 to 4 large garlic bulbs
2 tablespoons olive oil
Salt and freshly ground
   black pepper
2 bay leaves
1 large carrot, diced
1 small onion, cut into
   wedges
2 large glasses of red
   cooking wine

1. Preheat the oven to 375°C.

2. Place the chopped celery, 1 sprig of each herb and a handful of unpeeled garlic cloves into the chicken cavity.

3. Place half the remaining cloves in a lidded casserole, put the chicken on top, brush with olive oil and season well. Arrange the bay leaves, carrot, onion, and remaining herbs and garlic cloves around the chicken.

4. Drizzle with olive oil then pour over the red wine. Cover and roast for at least 1 hour 20 minutes, or until the chicken is tender and the juices run clear when the flesh is pierced with a skewer.

5. Either serve with toasted bread, spread with the soft flesh of the garlic cloves, or blend the garlic flesh with the juices from the bottom of the casserole to make a creamy sauce.

SLOW LAMB WITH YOGURT MINT SAUCE

Don't be put off by the long cooking time for this dish. It's incredibly quick and easy to prepare, and slow roasting allows the meat to become tender as well as giving fantastic flavor. You can leave it to cook overnight or prepare it in the morning for supper.

Serves 4 to 6

4 pounds shoulder of lamb
Salt and freshly ground
   black pepper
2 tablespoons olive oil
3 onions, sliced
4 carrots, quartered
   lengthwise
1 garlic bulb or 8 to 10 cloves,
   peeled and left whole
1 bay leaf
1 cup white wine
1 cup vegetable, beef or
   chicken stock

For the sauce
3 tablespoons plain yogurt
2 sprigs of fresh mint,
   leaves only
Sea salt and freshly
   ground black pepper

1. Preheat the oven to 250°F.

2. Season the lamb well with salt and freshly ground black pepper.

3. Heat the olive oil in a large roasting pot on high heat. Add the lamb joint to the roasting pot and fry for about 15 minutes, turning regularly, until browned all over. Turn down the heat.

4. Add the vegetables, garlic cloves, and bay leaf around the meat, then pour in the wine and stock. Bring to a boil before placing the casserole in the oven. Cook for up to 7 hours. (Although the meat will be cooked after about 5 hours, it's best left for the full time if possible.) Turn the meat halfway through cooking.

5. Remove the pot from the oven and transfer the lamb and vegetables to a serving dish. Cover with foil and return to the oven to keep warm.

6. To make the sauce, skim off any excess fat from the liquid in the pot, then place the pot on the stove top on medium heat. Boil until the liquid has reduced by about a quarter, then add the yogurt and mint leaves, stirring well. Reduce the heat so the sauce comes to a simmer, remove the mint leaves, and add seasoning if needed.

7. Pour the sauce into a gravy pot and serve the lamb with mashed potatoes and a steamed green vegetable.

MUSHROOM PIZZA

Homemade pizza is as satisfying to prepare as it is to eat. This recipe is a recreation of a mouth-watering pizza I was served in Verona. It has no tomato sauce, which means it's even quicker to make—and you'll be surprised that you don't even miss it. Serve with mixed greens.

Makes 2 large pizzas

For the base
4 cups plain flour, plus extra for dusting
1 packet (¼-ounce) fast-acting (or instant) yeast
2 tablespoons olive oil
2 teaspoons sugar or honey

For the topping
¾ pound porcini or other flavorful mushrooms, sliced
A few sprigs of fresh rosemary, finely chopped
4 garlic cloves, peeled
Olive oil
Salt and freshly ground black pepper
1 cup buffalo mozzarella, chopped
¼ cup grated Parmesan

1. To make the base, mix the flour and yeast in a large bowl and make a well in the center. In a jug, mix the olive oil and sugar or honey with 1¼ cups of warm water, then pour into the well of the flour mixture and gradually mix to form a soft and slightly sticky dough.

2. Transfer the dough to a lightly floured counter and lightly flour your hands. Knead the dough by hand for at least 10 minutes, until smooth and pliable. Place the dough back in the bowl and cover with oiled plastic wrap. Let rise for 45 minutes or until doubled in size.

3. Preheat the oven to 400°F.

4. Place the mushrooms and chopped rosemary sprigs into a bowl. Crush in the garlic, pour over 2 to 3 tablespoons of olive oil, season with salt and freshly ground pepper and combine well.

5. Remove the plastic wrap from the dough and divide it into two balls. On a lightly floured counter, carefully stretch them out into round bases about ¼ inch thick.

6. Cover each base with the mushroom mixture then top with mozzarella and Parmesan.

7. Bake the pizzas in the oven until the bases are crisp and golden-brown around the edges and the cheese has melted.

ROASTED BUTTERNUT SQUASH RISOTTO *VEGETARIAN

As well as being sweet and delicious, butternut squash is packed with vitamins and minerals, adding an extra health kick to this vegetarian dinner.

Serves 4

1 large butternut squash, cut into large chunks, seeds removed
3 to 4 large garlic cloves, peeled
1 tablespoon olive oil, plus extra for drizzling
A few sprigs of thyme, plus 1 tablespoon chopped thyme
Salt and freshly ground black pepper
¼ cup butter
1 large onion, finely chopped
1 cup Arborio risotto rice
½ cup white wine
4 cups vegetable stock
A handful of freshly grated vegetarian Parmesan, plus extra to serve
A handful of toasted pine nuts, to serve

1. Preheat the oven to 375°F.

2. Place the butternut squash in a large bowl, then crush in 1 to 2 garlic cloves, drizzle with olive oil, throw in the thyme sprigs, and season well. Mix thoroughly, ensuring the squash gets a good covering of oil and the garlic is well distributed. Put the mixture in a large roasting pan and roast for 30 to 40 minutes, or until the edges of the squash begin to brown.

4. Remove the squash from the oven and allow it to cool slightly before scraping the flesh away from the skin into a bowl, removing any thyme twigs. Scrape any sticky juices into the bowl and mash the squash. Keep warm while making the risotto.

5. Heat the olive oil and 2 tablespoons of butter in a heavy-based pan, add the onion, and gently fry until softened, about 2 minutes. Crush in two garlic cloves and gently fry for another 2 minutes.

6. Add the rice and stir well so the grains become coated in the butter and oil. Pour in the wine and stir well until absorbed.

7. Add a ladleful of hot stock and stir until absorbed. Keep the pan simmering while gradually adding more stock and continuing to stir, until the rice is cooked al dente, about 15 to 20 minutes. The risotto should have a smooth and creamy consistency. Add more stock if necessary.

8. Remove from the heat and add the mashed squash, grated Parmesan, 2 tablespoons of butter, 1 tablespoon of chopped thyme, and seasoning to taste. Stir well.

9. Serve with toasted pine nuts and a sprinkling of grated or shaved Parmesan.

SPAGHETTI CARBONARA

Pasta sauces lend themselves particularly well to the addition of garlic. There are several ways of preparing this Italian favorite, but my recipe includes using extra garlic for enhanced flavor and health benefits.

Serves 4

1 tablespoon olive oil
6 thick slices of pancetta or bacon, chopped into small pieces
4 shallots, finely diced
4 fat garlic cloves, finely chopped
4 large eggs
½ cup freshly grated Parmesan
Freshly ground black pepper
1 pound fresh spaghetti
2 scallions, chopped
A handful of fresh basil leaves, chopped
A handful of fresh parsley leaves, chopped

1. Heat the oil in a large frying pan on medium heat and gently fry the pancetta, shallots, and garlic for 5 to 7 minutes, or until the shallots have softened.

2. In a bowl, lightly beat the eggs and most of the grated Parmesan, reserving a little for the garnish. Season with freshly ground black pepper.

3. Boil the pasta in a large pan of salted boiling water according to packet instructions, about 2 to 3 minutes.

4. Drain the cooked spaghetti, then return it to the pan, off the heat. Quickly add the pancetta, shallots, and garlic and pour in the egg mixture, stirring well.

5. Add the scallions, basil, and parsley, and stir well again.

6. Serve immediately, sprinkled with freshly ground black pepper and extra Parmesan.

When sautéing garlic, take great care to make sure it never turns more than pale gold to light brown in color and never allow it to turn dark brown as this will impair the flavor. If you wish to keep the garlic flavors subtle, it is best to lightly sauté the garlic very briefly in oil then, before it can turn brown, allow it to simmer with the juices of the other ingredients.

ASIAN FISH PARCEL

A magical trio of flavors—chile, garlic and ginger—works particularly well in this quick and simple fish dinner, which can be made using fresh or frozen fish.

Serves 4

Olive oil
4 large fillets of pollack, or
   other sustainable white fish
A thumb-sized piece of
   ginger, peeled and grated
8 garlic cloves, sliced
2 red chiles, finely sliced
¼ cup light soy sauce
½ tablespoon toasted
   sesame oil
2 bok choy, finely sliced
2 scallions, finely chopped,
   to garnish
A handful of fresh cilantro,
   coarsely chopped,
   to garnish
1 cup steamed jasmine
   rice, to serve

1. Preheat the oven to 350°F.

2. Take four sheets of aluminum foil, large enough to loosely encase each fillet, and lay on a counter. Brush one side of each sheet with olive oil.

3. Place a fish fillet in the center of each sheet then arrange on a baking tray, bringing the sides of the sheets up around the fish.

4. Top each fillet with the ginger, garlic, chile, and soy sauce, then fold over the foil to seal. Transfer the tray to the oven and bake the parcels for 15 to 20 minutes. In the meantime, lightly sauté the bok choy in sesame oil for 3 to 4 minutes on medium heat.

5. Serve the fish on a bed of jasmine rice alongside the bok choy with the juices from the parcels and garnished with chopped cilantro and scallions.

SPICY BEEF
& SCAPES STIR-FRY
*DAIRY-FREE

Garlic scapes bring a fantastic crunchy texture with fresh garlic flavors to all sorts of dishes.

Serves 4

2 tablespoons light soy sauce
A thumb-sized piece of
   ginger, peeled and grated
1 small red chile
1 teaspoon sesame oil
2 large garlic cloves
1 pound sirloin steak, cut
   into thin strips
1 cup garlic scapes (or
   scallions or garlic chives),
   cut into 2-inch lengths
2 tablespoons sunflower oil
1 red pepper, sliced
¼ cup hot beef stock
1 cup steamed white rice,
   to serve

1. Combine the soy sauce, ginger, chile, and sesame oil in a bowl. Crush in the garlic and add the steak, tossing to coat it completely. Let it stand for 15 minutes.

2. Blanche the scapes for 2 minutes in salted boiling water, then drain and set aside.

3. Heat the oil in a wok and, on high heat, fry the steak strips in two batches for about 2 minutes each. The meat should be browned on the outside but still pink in the middle. Heat the rest of the oil in the wok, add the red pepper and fry for a minute or so, then add the scapes, all the steak, any remaining juices from the marinade, and the stock and stir-fry until piping hot. Serve immediately on plain rice.

The scape is the generic name for a flower stalk that emerges from the top of the plant, sometimes twisting and curling before growing straight up.

TANDOORI CHICKEN

This delicious Indian dish wouldn't be the same without garlic adding heat to the spicy yogurt marinade.

Serves 4

8 chicken thighs, drumsticks
   or 4 breasts, skinned
Pinch of salt
Juice of 1 lemon
A thumb-sized piece of
   ginger, peeled and grated
6 garlic cloves, minced
2 green chiles, finely chopped
2 teaspoons garam masala
2 teaspoons sumac
¼ cup plain yogurt
2 tablespoons butter

To serve
Juice of 1 lemon
1 red onion, finely sliced
Salt and freshly ground
   black pepper
2 handfuls of fresh mint
   leaves
¼ cup plain yogurt
Flatbread

1. Cut a few incisions into the chicken pieces using a small, sharp knife. Place the chicken into a bowl then sprinkle over the salt, lemon juice, and all the spices, massaging into the chicken until well coated.

2 Add ¼ cup of yogurt and mix with the chicken and spices. Cover and refrigerate overnight or for a minimum of 4 hours.

3. Preheat the oven to its highest setting.

4. Remove the chicken pieces from the yogurt and lay them in a roasting pan or on a baking tray, making sure they have plenty of room. Roast in the center of the oven for 20 minutes. Halfway through cooking, add a knob of butter on top of the chicken to give it a nice browned finish.

5. Remove the chicken from the oven and let rest for 5 minutes.

6. To serve, squeeze the lemon juice over the onion slices and season. Pile the dressed onion and mint leaves onto a plate with the tandoori chicken and accompany with yogurt and flatbread on the side.

SPICY CHICKPEA & BROCCOLI CURRY

*GLUTEN-FREE *DAIRY-FREE

Not all curries include vast quantities of garlic, but many certainly benefit from the great base flavors it creates. Frying crushed garlic and ginger together is one of my favorite ways to start a curry dish. This one is delicious, healthy and economical, and I always find it tastes even better the day after I've made it.

Serves 4

2 tablespoons olive oil
1 onion, finely chopped
6 garlic cloves, minced
A thumb-sized piece of
   ginger, grated
2 red chiles, deseeded and
   finely chopped
1 teaspoon turmeric
1 teaspoon ground cumin
2 teaspoons ground cilantro
1 teaspoon garam masala
2 × 14½-ounce cans chickpeas
1 × 14½-ounce can chopped
   tomatoes
1/3 cup red lentils
½ cup coconut cream
1 head of broccoli, chopped
   into small florets
Sea salt and freshly ground
   black pepper

To serve

2 handfuls of fresh
   cilantro, chopped
1 cup brown rice, cooked

1. Heat the olive oil in a deep saucepan or a wok and fry the onion, garlic, ginger, and chiles on medium heat for 2 minutes.

2. Add the spices and fry for another 5 minutes, adding more oil if necessary.

3. Pour in the chickpeas and tomatoes, add the lentils and coconut cream, then simmer until the lentils have softened.

4. Add the broccoli and simmer for another 5 minutes, then season to taste.

5. Garnish with a sprinkling of cilantro and serve with the brown rice.

Pairing ginger and garlic is one of the building blocks of Indian cuisine and ginger-garlic paste is an indispensable ingredient in many condiments and curries. You make it with equal quantities of garlic and ginger, blended together, and Indian cooks often make up huge batches as it's something they can guarantee they'll be using every day.

DIPS, SAUCES & DRESSINGS

AIOLI

This extremely versatile garlic mayonnaise is originally from the Provence region in the south of France, which helps explain the origin of the name. Ail is the French word for garlic and "oli" is from the Latin oleum, meaning oil. It works equally well served as a dip with steamed vegetables or as a sauce to accompany fish or meat.

Makes about 350ml

3 large garlic cloves, peeled
2 medium egg yolks
1 tablespoon Dijon mustard
1 cup olive oil
Juice of ¼ lemon
Salt and freshly ground
   black pepper

1. Using a pestle and mortar, crush the garlic with a pinch of salt to form a paste.

2. In a bowl, whisk the garlic, egg yolks, and mustard together.

3. Add the olive oil in a steady pour and whisk until all the oil is absorbed and the mixture has thickened.

4. Add the lemon juice and season to taste. If you'd like to use the aioli as a sauce, whisk in a few drops of warm water to make it runnier.

CLASSIC HUMMUS

We serve this hummus in our café and the bowl is always returned as if it's been licked clean. Need I say more?

Serves 4

1 × 14½-ounce can chickpeas, drained
Juice of ½ lemon
1 heaping teaspoon cumin
3 garlic cloves, minced
1 tablespoon chopped cilantro
2 teaspoons tahini
2 to 3 tablespoons olive oil
Large pinch of salt and freshly ground black pepper

1. Place all the ingredients in a food processor and blend. To keep a thicker texture, don't blend for too long.

2. Serve with any combination of crudités, breadsticks, or warmed pita bread.

VINAIGRETTE

The use of sunflower oil instead of olive oil makes this dressing much lighter, making it the perfect partner for a crunchy green salad. Freshly made vinaigrette will keep in a jar for up to a week, or in a sealed container in the refrigerator for several weeks.

Makes about ½ cup

2 tablespoons white wine
   vinegar
¼ cup sunflower oil
1 teaspoon Dijon mustard
1 garlic clove, minced
Sea salt and freshly ground
   black pepper

1. Put the vinegar, oil, mustard, and garlic in a screw-top jar and season. Cover the jar and shake well to combine.

2. Store in a cool place until ready to use, adding fresh herbs just before serving if desired.

GARLIC & CILANTRO YOGURT DRESSING

This dressing will keep in a sealed container in the refrigerator for about three days.

Makes about ½ cup

¼ cup plain yogurt
Juice of ¼ lemon
A ¼-inch-sized piece of
   ginger, peeled and grated
1 garlic clove, minced
Small handful of fresh
   cilantro, coarsely
   chopped

1. Mix all the ingredients in a bowl.

TZATZIKI *VEGETARIAN *GLUTEN-FREE

One of my all-time favorites. Some recipes suggest salting the cucumber to remove excess moisture, but personally I don't think this is necessary if you use very fresh, crisp cucumbers and serve the dip right away. In my experience, there are never any leftovers!

Makes about 1¾ cups

½ large cucumber
2 garlic cloves
1 cup thick Greek yogurt
½ cup crème fraîche
1 tablespoon each finely chopped parsley and mint
1 tablespoon olive oil
Juice of ¼ lemon
Salt and freshly ground black pepper

1. Peel, deseed, and finely dice the cucumber and crush the garlic. Stir all the ingredients together, adjusting the seasoning if necessary, then spoon into a serving bowl and garnish with a sprinkle of chopped mint.

2. Serve as an appetizer or snack with crudités (batons of raw carrot, celery, etc.), toasted pita bread, or crisps. Alternatively, tzatziki makes a refreshing side to sizzling lamb chops.

MOROCCAN DRESSING *VEGETARIAN *GLUTEN-FREE *DAIRY-FREE

This dressing will keep in a sealed container in the refrigerator for a week (photo on page 79).

Makes about ¾ cup

½ cup extra virgin olive oil
3 tablespoons red wine vinegar
1 teaspoon sweet paprika
½ teaspoon ground cumin
1 garlic clove, finely chopped
Small handful of fresh flat-leaf parsley, finely chopped

1. Mix all the ingredients in a bowl until well combined.

PICKLED GARLIC, LEMON, & LIMES

*VEGETARIAN *GLUTEN-FREE

Delicious homemade pickles have long been a favorite in our family, which is why we make and sell a huge range of pickles and chutneys. And as we're constantly coming up with new creations, our range is growing by the year. This recipe is a real winner. I've chosen to share it in this book because it's very easy to make at home, unlike some of our recipes that require a long list of ingredients and much more preparation time.

Makes 1 jar

3 tablespoons mustard seeds
1 tablespoon fenugreek seeds
2 tablespoons peanut oil,
  for frying
1 teaspoon turmeric
1 tablespoon red chile powder
3 unwaxed lemons, cut into
  small chunks
3 unwaxed limes, cut into
  small chunks (rinds on,
  seeds discarded)
2 garlic bulbs, cloves peeled
3 tablespoons sea salt

1. Using a pestle and mortar, crush the mustard and fenugreek seeds.

2. Heat the oil in a pan and gently fry all the spices for 2 minutes, then add the fruit, garlic cloves, and salt. Stir and remove from the heat.

3. Place the mixture in a sterilized airtight container or jar. Try to choose a container that doesn't leave too much air when filled with the mixture.

4. Leave to mature in the refrigerator for at least 10 days, turning occasionally.

CUCUMBER KIMCHI

*DAIRY-FREE

The Koreans have been eating this incredibly healthy dish with almost every meal for centuries, the earliest references to Kimchi being from at least 2,600 years ago. It is made with fermented vegetables, usually cabbage, combined with many flavors and spices, including garlic. Here is a cucumber-based version which is relatively easy to prepare and the crispy crunch of the cucumber combined with garlic and chili taste delicious.

Makes 1 large batch, enough for 2 large jars

1½ pounds small cucumbers (pickling cucumbers work best but large cucumbers also work)
2 tablespoons sea salt
½ onion, finely chopped
4 scallions, sliced lengthwise then chopped diagonally
4 garlic cloves
1 small red chile, deseeded and finely chopped (optional)
1 to 2 tablespoons Korean chile pepper powder, gochugaru (or any red chile powder)
2 teaspoons honey
2 teaspoons vinegar

1. Wash and chop the cucumbers into 2-inch long pieces.

2. Place them in a large ceramic bowl and sprinkle with the salt, then leave at room temperature overnight or at least for a few hours.

3. Add the onion and scallions to the cucumber, crush in the garlic cloves, and then add the chile, chile powder, honey, and vinegar. Mix all the ingredients together well.

4. Place the mixture in the refrigerator to cool. When cooled, you can eat this immediately. Alternatively, transfer into two large sterilized jars, and leave it to ferment at room temperature for a couple of days before putting it in the refrigerator. As the cucumbers will eventually lose their crunch, it is best to eat this kimchi within a week or so.

The beauty of this side dish or *banchan*, as the Koreans call it, is that it not only livens up your palate but is also the key to maintaining a healthy digestive system thanks to the presence of gut-friendly bacteria, *lactobacillus*. Western diets typically lack fermented foods and many would argue that this is of great detriment to our health.

HOT TOMATO SALSA *DAIRY-FREE

One of our best-selling relishes is a very hot tomato and garlic salsa called Vampire Relish. This is a variation that uses fresh tomatoes and will definitely ensure no fanged friends dare come to your party.

Serves 12 to 16

4 large vine-ripened
   tomatoes, coarsely chopped
½ red onion, coarsely chopped
2 garlic cloves, chopped
Juice of 1 lime
2 teaspoons dried chile flakes
2 teaspoons chile sauce
   (e.g. Tabasco), or to taste
1 tablespoon red wine vinegar
Salt and freshly ground
   black pepper, to taste
A few sprigs of fresh parsley,
   finely chopped

1. Place all the ingredients, except the parsley, in a food processor. Blend carefully to keep the mixture chunky.

2. Stir in the parsley, season to taste, and refrigerate until needed. It tastes better if left for a couple of hours before serving with tortilla chips.

This classic pesto recipe and variation offer a simple yet delicious way of introducing more garlic into your diet—I'm always generous with the garlic, so you may vary the quantities to suit your taste. The sauce can be stirred into freshly cooked pasta, added to sandwiches or bruschetta, mixed into bean salads, spread over roasted meats, or used as stuffing for chicken breasts.

CLASSIC PESTO *GLUTEN-FREE

2 tablespoons pine nuts
Large bunch of fresh basil leaves
2 large garlic cloves, peeled
½ cup olive oil
Juice of ¼ lemon
2 tablespoons grated Parmesan
Sea salt

1. Lightly toast the pine nuts in a frying pan, until they are pale golden brown.

2. Put the toasted pine nuts and remaining ingredients, except the Parmesan, in a food processor and pulse until the desired consistency is reached—I prefer pesto to have a little texture.

3. Stir in the grated Parmesan and add salt to taste.

GREEN GARLIC PESTO *GLUTEN-FREE

3 large green garlic bulbs, roots removed
2 garlic cloves, chopped
¼ cup olive oil
1 teaspoon salt
¼ cup mixed seeds (pine nuts, pumpkin seeds, and sunflower seeds)
A good handful of fresh basil leaves
1¾ cups finely grated Parmesan or pecorino
Sea salt

1. Finely chop the bulbs, stems, and leaves.

2. Place all the ingredients, except the cheese, in a food processor and pulse until you reach the desired consistency.

3. Stir in the cheese and add salt to taste. Mix in more olive oil if the pesto is too dry.

THE BEST WHOLE ROASTED GARLIC

*VEGETARIAN *DAIRY-FREE *GLUTEN-FREE

We've tried and tested so many different ways of roasting garlic at home and in our farm café. After much deliberation, this is our recommended method for the most succulent, juicy, sweet cloves. You can serve the whole bulb alongside roasted meats.

Makes 1 per person

1 whole garlic bulb
  per person
Olive oil

1. Preheat the oven to 350°F.

2. Cover the outside of the bulb(s) in olive oil. Loosely wrap them in aluminum foil (you can use a roasting pot if you have one) then roast in the oven for 1 hour.

3. Unwrap the aluminum foil or remove the lid of the roasting pot and roast uncovered for another 10 minutes.

4. To serve, slice the bulb horizontally; making a kind of lid that can be lifted up to spoon out the soft flesh of the cloves.

INDEX

Moroccan dressing 81
mushrooms: immunity-boosting
    soup 22
    mushroom pizza 59

N

noodles: Vietnamese chicken
    broth 21

O

oak-smoked garlic dauphinoise 36
onions: garlic, onion, & thyme
    frittata 29
oyster mushrooms: immunity-
    boosting soup 22

P

pancetta: spaghetti carbonara 63
papaya: som tam 43
pasta: spaghetti carbonara 63
peanuts: som tam 43
peeling garlic 8
pesto: classic pesto 86
    green garlic pesto 86
pickled garlic, lemon, & limes 82
pine nuts: classic pesto 86
pizza, mushroom 59
pomegranates: warm lentil &
    halloumi salad 44
porcini mushrooms: immunity-
    boosting soup 22
    mushroom pizza 59
potatoes: garlic, onion, & thyme
    frittata 29
    oak-smoked garlic dauphinoise
    36
    roasted garlic potatoes 39

R

relishes: hot tomato salsa 85
risotto, roasted butternut squash 60
rosemary: garlic & rosemary focaccia 47

S

salad, warm lentil & halloumi 44
salsa, hot tomato 85
sauces: aioli 74
    yogurt mint sauce 57
seafood: avocado garlic shrimp 30
seeds: green garlic pesto 86
shiitake mushrooms: immunity-
    boosting soup 22
shrimp, avocado garlic 30
slicing garlic 8
som tam 43
soups: gazpacho 25
    immunity-boosting soup 22
    Vietnamese chicken broth 21
spaghetti carbonara 63
sprouting broccoli, spicy 40
stir-fry, spicy beef & scapes 67
storing garlic 11
sulphur compounds 10, 11

T

tandoori chicken 68
tarts: garlic & tomato tarte tatin 14
thyme: garlic, onion, & thyme
    frittata 29
tomatoes: bruschetta 26
    garlic & tomato tarte tatin 14
    garlic bloody Mary 18
    gazpacho 25
    hot tomato salsa 85
    som tam 43
    spicy chickpea & broccoli curry 71
tzatziki 81

V

vegetarian dishes: aioli 74
    the best cheesy garlic bread 48
    the best whole roasted garlic 89
    classic hummus 77
    garlic & cilantro yogurt
        dressing 78
    garlic & rosemary focaccia 47
    garlic & tomato tarte tatin 14
    garlic bloody Mary 18
    garlic, cumin & beet fritters 32
    garlic, onion & thyme frittata 29
    gazpacho 25
    immunity-boosting soup 22
    Moroccan dressing 81
    oak-smoked garlic dauphinoise 36
    pickled garlic, lemon & limes 82
    roasted butternut squash risotto 60
    tzatziki 80
    vinaigrette 78
    warm lentil & halloumi salad 44
Vietnamese chicken broth 21
vinaigrette 78
vodka: garlic bloody Mary 18

Y

yogurt: garlic & cilantro yogurt
    dressing 78
    slow lamb with yogurt mint
        sauce 57
    tzatziki 81

Z

zucchini: zucchini fritters 31
    warm lentil & halloumi salad 44

WITH THANKS

To all my tasters and testers of everything from the sweet and delicious to the extremely experimental.

Special thanks to my husband, Barnes, for his unfailing support and my children Arlo and Freya for already being able to recognize a good garlic bulb.

To my dear friend and excellent cook, Columbine Mulvey, for all her expert help, culinary tips, ideas, and inspiration.

To my parents, without whom this book would not have been possible, for so many reasons other than the obvious. Thank you both.

To Kyle, Judith, and Vicki at Kyle Books for all their hard work and their faith in this book.

To everyone at The Garlic Farm. Keep up the good work!

This condensed edition published in 2016
by Kyle Books
www.kylebooks.com

First published in Great Britain in 2012
under the title *Garlic: The Mighty Bulb*

Distributed by National Book Network
4501 Forbes Blvd, Suite 200,
Lanham, MD 20706
Phone: (800) 462-6420
Fax: (800) 338-4550
customercare@nbnbooks.com

10 9 8 7 6 5 4 3 2 1

ISBN 978-1-909487-55-0

Project Editor: Claire Rogers
Designer: Helen Bratby
Photographer: Peter Cassidy
Illustrator: Jenni Desmond
Food and Props Stylist: Annie Rigg
Production: Nic Jones and Gemma John

Library of Congress Control No.:
2016939830

Color reproduction by ALTA London
Printed and bound in China by C&C Offset
Printing Co., Ltd.

* Note: all eggs are free-range